Dear Herb,

My Best
Always.

Jim Hodgson
1992

AMERICAN SENRYU

AMERICAN SENRYU

Verses by a former ambassador

JAMES D. HODGSON

The Japan Times

ISBN4-7890-0661-1 C0095
AMERICAN SENRYU—Verses by a former ambassador—
Copyright © 1992 by James Day Hodgson
First edition: October 1992

Cover art: Fumio Kaminaga
Published by The Japan Times, Ltd.
5-4, Shibaura 4-chome, Minato-ku, Tokyo 108, Japan
Printed in Japan

Contents

Foreword   *7*
Preface   *9*
Japan: Fascination with Form   *11*
Senryu Through the Ages   *17*
Ambassadorial Verses   *27*
Reflections   *29*
Observations   *63*
On the Writing of These Verses   *87*
How I Came to Write "Humor"   *90*

Bibliography   *95*

Foreword

It is a privilege for me to introduce *American Senryu—Verses by a former ambassador*—by James Hodgson, which is one of the best works that I know on the Japanese distinctive verse form of Senryu.

I have known Ambassador Hodgson for many years, particularly since he came to Japan as U.S. Ambassador in 1974. I became the Japanese Foreign Minister later that year, and enjoyed working with him for nearly two years. The period of his service in Japan (1974–77) is marked by some of the monumental events in the history of the Japan-U.S. relationship: President Ford paid the first official visit to Japan as incumbent U.S. President. In October the following year, Their Imperial Majesties Emperor Hirohito and Empress Nagako visited the United States for the first time after the War. The relationship between our two nations was entering a new era of closer partnership. Ambassador Hodgson, with the great help of Mrs. Hodgson, contributed enormously to ensuring the success of these historic events. I look back on those hectic and enlightening years with a sense of deep gratitude and respect for his devoted work and rare talents.

Besides his professional accomplishments as a senior diplomat, his knowledge and insatiable interests in Japanese art and culture would always impress me. He even owned some rare pieces of venerable Japanese artists like Hiroshige and Hokusai, and was extremely well versed in their arts. I should confess, however, that little have I known till recently that he has such appreciation for Senryu. Senryu, as he writes in this book, is a creation of the early eighteenth century. It is known as satirical literature that deals with the joys and sorrows of popular life, the realities of human nature, and social establishments. Having read the book, I was truly fascinated with his insightful analysis and with his work.

Mutual understanding is essential in solidifying the bond of trust between peoples of differnt backgrounds. For anyone wishing to gain fresh insight into the Japanese culture and literature, this book will provide an important clue to understanding where the Japanese people and its society come from. At the same time, Japanese readers will gain a new perspective on their own culture and will be impressed with the English form of Senryu, which retains its original relish intact.

I wish to congratulate Ambassador Hodgson on this superb work, which, I believe, will be treasured by many people around the world.

KIICHI MIYAZAWA
Prime Minister of Japan

Preface

Years ago, American commentator Upton Close wrote that the Japanese excel in one special type of humor. He said: "In their portrayal of the ridiculous, in assembling the incongruous, in exaggeration of human foibles, the Japanese are supreme."

Close was speaking of *Senryu* verse. Yet today few Americans are aware of this delightful form of Japanese literature, a form once cited by British scholar R.H. Blyth as "the most remarkable product of the Japanese mind."

In this book, I seek to introduce Senryu verse to a new audience and then to adopt its form, if not its content and tone, to reflect some thoughts gained while serving as ambassador to Japan.

JAMES D. HODGSON

Japan: Fascination with Form

An American who takes up residence in Japan must be prepared for a huge dose of culture shock. Yet along with some mystifying experiences, he will happily discover glorious new vistas of perception.

He will soon realize the commanding role proper form plays in Japan. For one thing, he will find himself gaining a new respect for the role *form* can play in enriching life. He will also understand that the mish-mash of styles and practices that Americans extol as pluralism holds little attraction for the men and women of Japan. In those people-packed islands there exists an explicitly preferred way to do or to say almost everything. Established patterns of behavior and speech—patterns nurtured and refined through the centuries—are rigorously observed. So *form* has emerged to become the essence of today's Japan.

To illustrate this, let us stand in the wings for a moment and listen to a Japanese notable as he delivers a traditional *aisatsu* (a short greeting offered at a public gathering). How will the audience judge their speaker? By his eloquence? No. By his histrionics? Never! He will be judged almost solely by whether he says exactly the right things in the right order while showing the right level of deference for his audience. The test will be one of form, not content.

Here, the contrast with the Western world is startling. With our insistence on naturalness and flexibility, we Americans are apt to be contemptuous of formal rigidities. With us, the battle between form and substance is a "no contest" affair. We not only opt for substance, we often clothe our preference in pretensions of virtue. With us, insistence on substance is "good"; emphasis on form is "bad."

Nonetheless, when in Japan, an American will find that form takes on luster. Only the crass can resist its appeal. Form is so omnipresent that it almost ceases to be contrasted with substance. Indeed, in a curious way, form seems to merge with substance. In classical Japanese literature and drama we discover many a theme where form clashes with substance. When these two lock horns, almost invariably substance comes off second best. Kurosawa's award-winning motion picture *Kagemusha* depicts just such a clash. The film offers an intriguing message: Established form, it suggests, even when bogus, can succeed where legitimate substance may fail.

During my three years as ambassador to Japan I came to the view that reliance on proper form plays a bonding role in Japanese society. Few societies function more smoothly. The Japanese have developed an astounding ability to get along well with one another; they probably do this better than any other people of our time. Observance of proper form in their daily lives strikes me as being a large part of the reason why.

* * *

The foregoing has been simply my way of leading up to some observations on one fascinating verse form found in Japanese literature, one called Senryu.*

Many Americans have become familiar with the Japanese verse known as Haiku. They know that Haiku features a seventeen-syllable, three-line verse structure, with the first and third lines having five syllables and the middle line, seven. Outside Japan, however, only a few aficionados are familiar with Senryu. Here is a verse identical in structure to that of Haiku, but wildly different in flavor and content.

Mandarins insist that the essential element of Haiku is refinement. Senryu, on the other hand, thumbs its nose at refinement. Yet it vastly surpasses Haiku in range and depth. For me, unvarnished realism marked the appeal of Senryu. Realism plus a bit of rascality. Senryu goes directly to the heart of the matter, even at times to the jugular. Enduring insights, often flavored with equally enduring humor, give Senryu a timeless quality.

Senryu's earthy realism, of course, denies its elegance. Reflecting a brazenly unsentimental look at life, Senryu verses range in taste from sensitive to vulgar. The illustrious British scholar of things Japanese, the late R.H.

---

*Named for one Karai Senryu (1718–90), now considered the father of Senryu verse and one of its earliest publishers (an incredible 167 volumes).

Blyth, praised Senryu as "the most remarkable product of the Japanese mind." One need not go quite that far overboard to appreciate this fascinating verse form, which, remarkably enough, often manages to shine through the fog of translation quite well.

Both Senryu's balanced form and its penetrating view of life attracted me. Its structure has an appearance comparable to that of the golden mean in the world of fine arts. For the ear, it offers cadence; for the eye, symmetry.

Does English literature feature anything comparable to Senryu? Not really. The closest approximation would be short satirical verse or perhaps the salty epigram. Yet neither has the rigidity of form nor all-seeing-eye flavor than mark Senryu.

During my years as the American ambassador in Tokyo, I came to regard this Japanese verse with great affection. Perhaps no form of literature is more adept at illuminating underexplored corners of the world's wisdom. Thus, I set about learning something of Senryu's history and its role in the current Japanese scene. The pages that immediately follow capsulize what I found.

AMERICAN SENRYU

Senryu Through the Ages

Edward Gibbon, author of *The Decline and Fall of the Roman Empire,* once observed that a people could not lay claim to being truly cultured until the passing of centuries gave them a strong sense of history. Given the newness of our new world, Americans have had little opportunity to nurture such a sensibility. Many of us, in fact, are inclined to dismiss history as something that happened to other people elsewhere. Perhaps only an American could have uttered Henry Ford's blunt "History is bunk!"

All this means that Americans are apt to react with surprise when they suddenly encounter an old-world view of history. This is exactly what happened to me in Tokyo. Within weeks of my Tokyo touchdown in mid-1974, I watched as an unfortunate incident triggered a dispute between Japan and its across-the-sea neighbor, the Republic of Korea. No more than a minor spat should have ensued. Yet ancient enmities between the two countries soon broke through the surface and a real hullabaloo erupted. Threats were exchanged. Tension filled the northeast Asian air.

"What will the United States do if Korea invades Japan?" Japanese officials implored of me.

"You can't be serious," was my reaction.

"But we are deadly serious," they snapped. "The Koreans tried to invade our islands once before you know."

"When?"

"In the thirteenth century," came the unblinking reply.

Finding people conditioned by events so remote in time leaves an American incredulous. Yet one eventually comes to realize that respect for their history and traditions extends all across the Japanese cultural landscape.

Certainly this pattern holds true of Japanese literature, the forms of which have a heritage that can be traced back almost unchanged and unchanging for hundreds of years. By Japanese standards, however, Senryu verse is something of a neophyte. It has been around only a little longer than the USA has been a nation. This finds Senryu still a struggling rookie in big-league competition that includes such venerable poetic structures as Haiku and Waka. Thus, many Japanese give a down-the-nose treatment to Senryu, somewhat as our Western Brahmins are apt to dismiss light verse. Britisher Kingsley Amis observes: "Light verse in English has neither the genealogical backing nor the distinguished patronage needed to make it wholly respectable." So it is with Senryu in Japan.

Yet Senryu's fledgling status is not the only hurdle it faces. Its penchant for realism gives many a Senryu verse an indelicate flavoring. Arbiters of Japanese taste show little appreciation for the raffish in literature. They would recoil at Cyril Connolly's suggestion that "vulgarity is the garlic in the salad of taste." Connolly, on the other hand, would relish the earthy flavor of many Senryu. Almost perversely, it turns out, literati of the Western world are often fond of the more pungent Senryu for the very reason Japanese mandarins spurn them.

Though still unranked with more classic forms of Japanese poetry, over the centuries Senryu verse has remained almost unvarying in form, content, and tone. These, of course, are standard ingredients of classicism. To me, Senryu clearly deserves to be regarded as "classic."

What, then, is Senryu actually all about? Mainly, it seeks to reflect and, indeed, at times to expose what is called "the human condition." Insight is its objective. A peek at life's little ironies, some glib word play, and even a touch of Zen are its tools. A Senryu verse will frequently evoke a mental flash that seems to "leave echoes in the mind." The mind's echoes, I find, are often accompanied by a nip at the funny bone.

Senryu verses are also rigorously impersonal. Never do we find an "I" in a Senryu verse. The writer remains wholly outside his creation—outside, aloof, and often anonymous. These, of course, are ingredients of mystique.

The nuance-rich Japanese language does nothing to minimize this mystique. Thus, we find the exquisitely constructed forms of their literature must always lose a good bit in translation. The translations used here perhaps lose more to nuance than they do to tenor of thought. Nor should one expect seventeen syllables in each translated verse.

Let me give a few examples of what I have been talking about. To start somewhere near the beginning of Senryu's history, perhaps we should hark back to Japan's illustrious seventeenth-century poet, Basho. About the time Shakespeare was offering his first sonnets to the world, Basho penned three now immortal lines. Today every Japanese school child is familiar with Basho's celebrated frog:

> *The old pond,*
> *A frog jumps in—*
> *The sound of water.* (JLCS)

This verse of Basho more nearly resembles Haiku than Senryu. Yet it does convey something of the flash imagery that came to mark many of the best Senryu.

Somewhat later Basho's disciple Kikaku showed a tougher strain of thought. As I see it, Kikaku laid the basis for the unvarnished realism that has become the core feature of Senryu. Note this gem:

> *He is a winter fly,*
> *Disliked*
> *But long lived.* (JLCS)

Though Senryu's delicious interplay of humanity and humor invades many an intimate scene and exposes many a shallow sentimentality, the subject matter is largely timeless. Note the following examples, circa A.D. 1760.

JLCS: *Japanese Life and Character in Senryu* by R.H. Blyth
OH: *Oriental Humor* by R.H. Blyth

On relations between the sexes:

> *The other woman*
> *Is not so mad on the husband*
> *As the wife is jealous.* (JLCS)

On the lure of lucre:

> *Whether you spend it*
> *Or whether you save it,*
> *Money **is** interesting.* (JLCS)

On life's ironies:

> *When the persimmon*
> *He planted finally bore fruit,*
> *His teeth had fallen out.* (JLCS)

Always skeptical, Senryu sees with a penetrating eye. Note the following:

> *Pretending to be asleep—*
> *Hah! The snore*
> *Is too regular.* (JLCS)

Nor is it taken in by wiles:

> *"Always thinking of you"*
> *And a lot of touching things—*
> *And then something about money.* (JLCS)

Senryu conspicuously lacks compassion for the weak:

> *The one who blubbered*
> *At the company meeting*
> *Was given the sack.* (JLCS)

Or for the silly:

> *The man who giggles*
> *Is omitted in the selection*
> *For the ambush.* (OH)

Though adept at exposing spurious sentiment, never does Senryu itself get sentimental. Even the ineffably sad is fair game:

> *"They are out," says the blindman,*
> *Admiring the plum blossoms*
> *With his nose.* (JLCS)

Certainly the rich and powerful are not spared:

> *His who's-who entry*
> *Doesn't say*
> *"Dances when drunk."* (JLCS)

Nor is the scholar given deference:

> *The chap who reads the classics*
> *Loses the argument*
> *About the rent.* (JLCS)

Even the final leveler is noted for what it is:

> *The width of the Styx*
> *Is just the same*
> *For rich and poor.* (JLCS)

Amazingly enough, a mere seventeen syllables can, at times, come up with something that borders on the metaphysical:

> *When we get down to*
> *The bottom of the bottom,*
> *Humanity is weeping.* (JLCS)

At other times when the philosophic yields to the poetic, a delightful fragment can emerge:

> *As if after thinking*
> *It over, a raindrop*
> *Falls.* (JLCS)

The poetic, in turn, may yield to avuncular advice:

> *Do not try to be made much of;*
> *Just be careful*
> *Not to be rejected.* (OH)

To many a literal-minded Westerner, some forms of Japanese literature at times seem intent on fuzzing up the obvious. But not Senryu. Senryu smacks us in the face with it. We often find ourselves confronted with a thought so obvious we wonder how we could have ignored it.

For instance, we may come upon lines like these:

> *Happiness*
> *Is less eloquent*
> *Than anger.*   (JLCS)

And we think—but of course!
Often our eyes have seen pictures not recorded by our mind, such as:

> *The morning haze—*
> *Heaven and earth*
> *Not yet divided.*   (JLCS)

Then we down-focus and find this:

> *The face of the grasshopper*
> *Looks like*
> *The face of the horse.*   (JLCS)

And how about this gem:

> *The nose—*
> *The nose only—*
> *Cannot laugh.*   (JLCS)

A nose can be laughed *at*, but of all our facial features, the nose alone is unmoved by mirth.

How often have we seen this person?

> *He is a fool—*
> *So he gets angry*
> *When he is made a fool of.* (JLCS)

Or someone who fits this picture:

> *After the greetings are over*
> *He becomes*
> *Cold-eyed again.* (JLCS)

I like the picture caught by this one:

> *If both are of a mind,*
> *Eyes are as eloquent*
> *As the lips.* (JLCS)

All of us are inclined to question the sincerity of gushing visitors. Note how this Senryu does it.

> *Until they are back*
> *On the ship, they praise Japan*
> *To the skies.* (JLCS)

When a Japanese strays into the Western world, things at variance with his own experience intrigue him. His attention may fix on a practice so much a part of our daily Western life that we never give it a second thought. Note this Senryu from the pen of a puzzled Japanese traveler:

> *A European meal;*
> *Every blessed dish and plate*
> *Is round!* (OH)

Obviously we Westerners are here seen as lacking in creativity. Perhaps we are. Our dishes are indeed almost uniformly (and in this Senryu "boringly") round. A gastronome treated to a dinner anywhere in Japan's enchanting archipelego will enjoy servings on dishes of nearly every shape—square, triangular, eliptical, pie-shaped, oval, and even, on occasion, round. For our dinnerware, we Westerners borrowed the term "China" from the Orient—yet we somehow neglected to acquire the Oriental taste for its multiple shapes. Why?

As with most differences between East and West, attempted explanations run the short gamut from inadequate to inane. We are left with the wonder of it all.

*   *   *

I have offered here but a sparse sampling of the thousands upon thousands of Senryu written through the centuries. I have hoped to suggest only a bit of their tantalizing flavor and range.

For personal reasons, perhaps one last Senryu deserves quoting:

> *If there is a margin*
> *In our lives,*
> *We write poetry on it.*   (JLCS)

To this charge I plead guilty. My verses herein serve as evidence.

Ambassadorial Verses

When Mrs. Hodgson and I flew into Tokyo's Haneda Airport in the sweltering summer of 1974, I was new to the world of diplomacy. Japan itself was largely unknown to me. Instantly, life became rich with novel experience. As the world is now beginning to learn, the Japanese are consummate hosts. They delight in introducing newcomers to their unique and intricate culture.

So, early on in Tokyo, for me two things came resoundingly together—a rash of intriguing experiences and exposure to a seductive new form of verse—Senryu. I could not resist the temptation to convert some impressions gained from the former into the attractive structure of the latter. Thus, this book.

But a warning is in order. Only the singular structure of Senryu—its seventeen-syllable structure—has been borrowed here. The content of my verse holds little similarity to the Japanese version.

The irony and imagery of home-grown Senryu springs from too deep within the wells of Japanese culture to be captured by an outsider. I believe that while the Western mind may appreciate, it cannot replicate, Japanese subtlety. So, sacrificing the flavor, I settled for pirating the form. Perhaps only the parentage remains intact, but I do not apologize for this borrowing!

No people have shown greater success in borrowing from others than the Japanese. They borrow with gusto and adapt with skill, constantly enriching their already stimulating milieu. All I have done with these verses of mine is to engage in a bit of reciprocity—to attempt a little reverse borrowing. So except in form, these verses of mine do not resemble Japanese Senryu. They do, however, reflect thoughts and insights gained during the illuminating years I spent in Japan.

Another warning. These verses of mine hold no pretense of Olympian significance.

My thought processes tend to graze over a lower landscape. I find myself uncomfortable when the verdant pastures of the intellect are fenced off from the uneven terrain of reality. In my approach to life I try to couple the two. I have sought to apply that approach here.

During the years of groping my way through diplomatic life in the Japanese cultural thicket, two distinct kinds of experiences emerged. One group prompted reflective thought, the other seemed to evoke flashes of insight. I sought to capture in my verse some of each. I call verses of the first group "Reflections"; those of the second, "Observations."

One final comment. I have done two things here that in more professional hands might be considered cheating. I have given a title to each of these verses and have added amplifying comments.

Reflections

TRUST

Should trust flow too deep,
When the channel grows shallow,
The craft will falter.

Yukichi Fukuzawa, Japan's versatile Meiji-period leader, saw trust as a towering virtue. "Trust supplies the oil needed to lubricate the machinery of human relationships," he wrote. I emphatically agree.

Yet in each relationship, whether between men or between nations, there exist limits to the level of trust that can wisely be extended. There are times, when out of an excess of goodwill or euphoria, or even out of miscalculation, these limits may be exceeded. The error may not immediately become apparent. Later, however, it can often erupt explosively, shattering the relationship.

The level of trust extended should reflect the degree of dependability of the relationship.

RHETORIC

*Fine words may translate
Readily to an alien tongue,
But not to wisdom.*

The world of diplomacy is almost shamefully glutted with eloquence. Words may please or inspire for the moment. Their flavor and point may even surmount translation. But to move them off page or podium into the heart and mind is another matter.

REALITY

In times of no bread,
The gods must despair giving
It to us daily.

Reality cannot be ignored, even by the deities. We should not ask the impossible of life. The gap between expectation and realization is perhaps the greatest cause of personal unhappiness in our time.

LICENSE

"Poetic license"—
The gift of the ungifted
To the most gifted.

"To them that hath shall be given." So the Good Book declares.

How unfair! Our egalitarian instincts are offended. Though it may upset our passion for equity, this biblical command endures because it reflects reality. We do indeed grant special privileges to the especially talented. We don't even require them to play by established rules.

Were a college freshman, for instance, to write "Something there is that doesn't love a wall," he would flunk elementary English composition. But then he is not Robert Frost.

CRITICISM

One of refined taste
May well extol earthiness—
A yokel may not.

Our credibility is often limited by who and what we are. Crudely expressed praise is particularly resented by the Japanese. Note how their resentment is expressed in this Japanese Senryu:

"Thunderin' good,"
Noisily praises
The uncouth visitor.   (JLCS)

EFFORT

*Our failure to please
Is less unfortunate than
Out failure to try.*

Reluctantly, life forces us to conclude that goodwill and determined effort are not always rewarded. Exhaustion or exasperation may at times tempt us to forsake both. Each of us personally, and the world community generally, will benefit if we resist succumbing to such temptation.

Success is, of course, our objective, but good intent validates all constructive effort.

HUMOR

The blackness of truth
Needs humor's illumination
To lighten one's life.

Though pursuit of truth is among man's most ennobling endeavors, the truth we may cherish in prospect often proves discouraging in aspect. So an antidote is needed. We find it in humor.

Humor provides two useful ingredients: for boredom it provides diversion; for wisdom, perspective. As used here, "lighten" carries an intended double meaning.

COMMUNICATION

A "disengagement,"
Says one. "Defeat" says another.
Yet acts are precise.

The finite world of action contrasts with the ambiguous world of words. Perspectives differ and man's mind is creative—thus, descriptions may vary. Yet the act itself stands as an incontrovertible fact.

This paradox induces a not infrequent contempt by men of action for men of words.

RISK

The edge of a cliff
Seems meant for looking over.
A man must do it.

Man is attracted to danger. So one must ask if what passes for a courageous act in the face of peril is often not merely an unthinking visceral response.

André Malraux doubted the merit of courage, dismissing it as "banal." Seneca tells us that courage is "greedy of danger" and hence is itself dangerous. Yet literature of all times and cultures extols courage as the one quality that separates great from lesser men.

Whether out of compulsion, caprice, or conviction, men do indeed take remarkable risks. We shall keep wondering why.

BEAUTY

*The exciting thought
That beauty is possible
Sustains us all.*

As seen here, beauty encompasses the full range of a sensually satisfying process—a process that starts with conception, extends into execution, and triumphs in realization. In this sense, such things as a well-played game, a complex business deal, or a successful diplomatic venture are all "beautiful."

In every sphere of activity, the prospect of a "beautiful" outcome is a powerful motivator of men.

MAN

*Man dreams, creates, loves—
What a remarkable creature!
We damn him overmuch.*

For the human intellect, the most elusive qualities seem to be scale, proportion, and possibility. To see things big, to see them in proper relation to each other and to see them in terms of reality, we must see things whole, not just in imperfect part.

Too often we concentrate on the imperfections of man. Unachievable standards become our yardstick. How silly.

When we view the whole man, not just his imperfections, he is far from the worthless creature portrayed by messianic prophets and minor poets.

The Japanese well understand the worth of man, as reflected in their aphorism: "Man is the ramparts. Man is the castle. Man is the moat."

RESULTS

*Words! page after page;
Endless ordering of facts.
By one act—muted.*

Here we note a familiar circumstance. Hours have been spent accumulating volumes of verbiage in an effort to make a case for some objective. Then we watch helplessly as a single swift action makes instantly obsolete or irrelevant all our carefully marshalled data—a classic illustration of the superiority of action over words in gaining ends.

LITURGY

Pure mumbo jumbo?
Or profound eternal truth?
A strange way to God!

The liturgy of another man's worship not only seems alien but curious, and often, even faintly ridiculous. Yet we find the liturgy of our own form of worship comforting.

Liturgy appeals more to man's emotional needs than to provide him a spiritual bridge to his creator. As such it serves a worthy but limited purpose. Here, form should *not* be mistaken for substance.

DIPLOMACY

*Cynics first dictum:
For persuasion to succeed,
Conceal the intent.*

Polls show that the title "Diplomat" draws a reaction of great respect among the public. How puzzling! From the time of Machievelli through Metternich and beyond, diplomacy has been associated with duplicity.

Can it be that the triumph of the diplomat lies in his ability to use tools associated with duplicity to fashion a humane result? Possibly.

HARMONY

*Lubricant among men;
Among nations—imperative!
Still unsought by fools.*

In Japan, harmony among men is an overriding value. Accordingly, a diplomatic touch ranks high among their sought-after virtues. The Western world is less appreciative—even at times cynical.

"To lead the life of a diplomat is to be constantly poised between a cliché and an indiscretion." So once observed that suave Briton, the late Harold Macmillan.

Nonetheless, when, through diplomacy, a seed of understanding can be sown successfully in discordant soil, the world rejoices.

IDENTITY

*The wise soon discover
That normalcy is indeed
The best path for life!*

In egocentric pursuit of an enhanced sense of self, some men do strange things. They indulge in affectation and posturing. The result: associates are repelled. Thus, such men are denied what they most seek—favorable attention. Recognition must be gained from a sounder base.

IGNORANCE

Flowing wide and deep
The world's flood of ignorance
Need engulf but fools.

The human energy expended battling ignorance is appalling. Is there no option other than a ceaseless struggle with this monster? Perhaps there may be.

Examine this possibility. What if some future Isaac Newton should discover a universal pattern with respect to earthly ignorance? The world's ignorance, he finds, is distributed outward equally in all directions from a central core of truth. This would, of course, mean that the ignorance on one side of an issue would cancel out the ignorance on the other.

My instincts like this idea. A life spent searching for a core of truth is clearly more rewarding than forever battling the world's unwisdom. At least I find it so.

ENEMIES

*The capacity
To gain the right enemies
Is part of genius.*

No man in his right mind deliberately sets out to make enemies. But few men of character and virility of thought can escape gaining some. In public life, a man is often respected as much for the disrepute of his enemies as for the worth of his friends. What holds true for men, holds true for nations.

ESSENCE

*Around the edges
Fuzziness is acceptable,
But not at the core.*

In a policy formulation, in a project plan, or even in a human relationship, we can accommodate a few peripheral loose ends. But unless the central substance has cohesion and point, trouble lies ahead. Murk has no place at the heart of things.

SUCCESS

Seeking more from life?
Recast your bell-shaped curve;
Set standards, not goals.

The wisdom of our time is rich in hokum. To get the most out of life, we are told, we should set goals. Goal achievement then becomes the measure of happiness. Goal failure, in turn, becomes seen as personal failure. How downright ridiculous!

Here another course is suggested. Personal attributes are distributed along a bell-shaped curve. Most of us will find that a few of our capabilities will rank near the top; the bulk will cluster near the middle, with another few mired down around the bottom.

For each of us this pattern suggests a twofold strategy. First, to seek a role in life where we can capitalize on our strong points and cushion our weaknesses. Second, to set high personal standards and let them, not pre-set objectives, guide our actions. Clinging to worthy standards, rather than chasing elusive goals, will serve to enhance our prospect of more fully enjoying the game called life.

HEDONISM

Ah, those shallow pools
Of sweet instant happiness—
Deep enough to drown.

In earlier days, Christians of predestination persuasion lived their lives as though they expected to live forever. Thus, matters of the moment were seen as matters of little consequence.

But in our century something has happened. The promised bliss of eternity has now been rejected in favor of more immediate joys. Today eternity seems too distant and immortality too dubious to warrant sacrifice. Pleasure deferred is seen as pleasure lost.

Yet life has its own Catch 22. The contemporary pursuit of instant gratification narrows life. So we now find ourselves awash in the nothingness of a no-tomorrow perspective.

PRIDE

*Perilous is pride—
Too little and man can't live,
Too much and he dies.*

Pride is a necessary nutrient for man's fragile ego. It stimulates attainment; it helps us absorb the shock of adversity. As Milton said, "Heaven is built on pride."

Yet East and West strongly agree on one thing—overweening pride destroys. Both Buddha and Aristotle so taught. The Greeks in fact gave us that useful word *hubris*—the wanton insolence that destroys the over-proud.

Philosophers in all ages and cultures excel at identifying human excesses. How to avoid those excesses is left up to us.

PETTINESS

A melange of evil
Swims noisily in the small mind
Before subsiding.

About all that can be said on behalf of the mean-spirited is that their fulminations are rarely rewarded. Most of their spiteful scheming sputters and peters out in pathetic ineptitude.

RESTRAINT

The ledger of life
Lists our charge for self-restraint
Under "accounts due."

When men give up one thing—no matter what it is—they do so to achieve but another. Much as we may admire self-denial, we come to realize that the self doing the denying usually has some ultimate reciprocity in mind.

Living involves an endless series of trade-off decisions. Judicious traders, not the meek, inherit the earth.

CHOICE

Inevitably,
Even in quest of noble virtue,
Gain involves loss.

Options exist. We must select. Selection requires rejection. That selected is rarely without its limitations. That rejected is rarely wholly lacking in worth.

Some lives are spent in a fruitless pursuit "to have it both ways." Nothing is more certain than the ultimate failure of such effort. The ability to live comfortably with one's tough decisions becomes a definition of maturity.

INNOCENCE

Ignored evil—
The price too often paid for
Purity of heart.

Absence of guile achieved by wearing mental blinders is a dubious virtue. The late British humorist Malcolm Muggeridge was deadly serious when he reminded us that purity of heart has a dangerous two-dimensional shallowness unless accompanied by penetrating perception. An uncorrupted heart must be coupled with a ruthless eye.

LIVING VS. LIFE

Vagaries of life
Lie well beyond man's control—
Not so its living.

Life's experiences are framed by forces that often lie outside our personal control. Yet by bringing our own *raison d'être* to living our lives, each of us can avoid entrapment of the human spirit by these forces. Forces that bear on life may inhibit. Living it our own way frees.

SEX

The mystery of sex
Lay beyond the Messiahs,
Even Christ and Buddha.

Should we crave guidance in sexual matters, the great prophets offer little help. Christ, it is generally believed, did not marry, and his teachings on the subject are wildly inexplicit.

Buddha took a wife and sired one child. But at age 29 he deserted both for a life of meditation, a questionable option available to few.

Mohammed, who had been orphaned early, not surprisingly married a mother-figure, a widow twice his age. Moses had a more "normal" marriage and his teachings are a bit more helpful, but only a bit.

Little wonder that ordinary men are so confused.

CIVILIZED MAN

*Control of instinct,
Man's first halting step toward
Civilization.*

Plato had it wrong. "Civilization began," he wrote, "when one man first persuaded another." Restraint of man's often unruly nature had to come first. Susceptibility to persuasion followed.

INTENT

*A "conspiracy"?
By whose rules shall acts be judged,
Doer or done to?*

Man craves order. He establishes rules. Different rules in different societies, of course. So when national interests clash, two things happen. Each judges the other by his own rules; each questions the legitimacy of the other's intent. Goodwill between nations then becomes sorely tested. To rise above insular shackles and preserve goodwill becomes the diplomat's challenge.

STIMULATION

We discover life's zest
Out on the dangerous edge
Where siren risk dwells.

The poet Browning wrote approvingly of "living on the dangerous edge of things." A contemporary sage suggests that man has three needs: identity, security, and stimulation. The schemes of social reformers often fail because they ignore man's need for stimulation. A risk-free society turns out to be an emotional graveyard. Mankind cannot abide the boredom.

DEATH

"Do not go gentle. . . ."
So pleads the youngish poet.
At times, the young amuse.

Dylan Thomas died young while his Welsh heart still beat the wild wonders of youth. Fate thus denied him the mellowing delights of advancing years.

    The more mature among us know better. When energy flags and tissues crumble, gentle is the *only* way to go.

Observations

ENIGMA

The world's other side—
Many wonders shown to her.
Her other side, unshown.

As seen here, even the exotic and sometimes puzzling Orient holds fewer mysteries than the Western woman who visits it.

Herewith, obviously, a pre-sexist observation is risked, one made hazardous, even obsolete, by contemporary sensitivities.

AGE 60

Now the "itis" age,
Arthr and burs, tendon and neur—
Even the names hurt!

Juvenal writes that old age brings with it a lamp. Metaphorically he is telling us that experience serves to illuminate understanding. A comforting thought.

Yet some oldsters might suggest that Juvenal's lamp could better be used to provide not light, but heat—heat to ease the pains of a deteriorating anatomy. Unfortunately, these turn out to be pains for which medical science provides names but not remedies.

To identify and name a problem without providing a remedy often masquerades as professionalism today.

LOVE

Endless is the need.
Short, the supply. We are left
Forever hungry.

Whether inscribed on ancient tablets or blared from today's stereos; whether writ by pen of prophet or poet—the plea, it seems, is always the same. The world, it is urged, is in need of more love.

One conclusion should become almost inescapable. Man craves love in amounts beyond that an imperfect universe can provide. Here we note a largely unacknowledged feature of what is ruefully called "the human condition." There is simply not enough love to go around! Sadly enough, the "supply and demand" equation seems to apply even to love.

If we could but realize that the copious love we each seek is indeed a limited commodity, perhaps then we would not demand so much of it. A less demanding mankind would be a giant step toward a less fractious world.

GRIEF

Barely dermis deep,
Set to gush from a newsprick,
Blood-tears of anguish.

We see here a person so compassionate, sensitive, and emotional that even slightly adverse news about a loved one prompts an instant eruption and outpouring of acute distress.

POLITICIAN

*Neat political feat—
Bullet-dodging artistry.
Sturdy? No. Nimble!*

For survival (i.e., re-election), the objective of a politician may shift from positive striving to avoidance of criticism. We may admire the deftness with which he does it, but we note what he sacrifices.

REACTION

Sad event; flat tone.
Stunned, calloused, or hurt?
You search for answers.

Some people write or talk with curious objectivity about a personal sorrow or tragedy suffered. How can they be so unemotional! You read or listen carefully to find clues to their true state of mind.

GOOD GUY

*First-rate heart paired with
Third-rate mind; tragic mark of
Creation's caprice.*

Sadly we learn that intellect is not always coincident with virtue. When, as at times occurs, we become acquainted with someone of high standards and human warmth who turns out to possess only a shallow cast of thought, we somehow feel cheated. It is difficult to combine affection with pity in a relationship.

BETWEEN THE LINES

Slight acquaintance writes;
Desired favor hidden somewhere.
You know it is there.

An unexpected letter from a distant acquaintance invariably signals he wants something. In contrast to straightforward correspondence among close friends, the acquaintance will often avoid too explicit a statement of his request. A close reading of his letter may be needed to discover what he really wants.

DEMENTIA

Luminous, those eyes;
Tragic glint of lunacy there?
The quaver confirms.

Shakespeare tells us the eyes mirror what lies behind them. There are encounters when we look into eyes that seem to reflect a hint of madness. And at times what we believe we may have seen in the eyes is verified by what we hear in speech. The voice tone signals we are in the presence of mental instability.

ROMANCE TODAY

The lens of the heart—
When its focus turns to "now,"
"Forever" gets lost.

Can anything enduring be expected of something called a "meaningful relationship"? Ugh! America's "now" generation often seems to treat marriage like Russian Roulette in reverse. Take a chance; if wedded life should happen to work out—great! If not, there's always next time.

When expectations are shallow, so is commitment. Would any writer today dare conclude a romantic tale with ". . . and they lived happily ever after?" Can't you hear the laughter!

FREE SPIRIT

Aimless psyche muses,
Arouses, explodes! Calm comes for one.
For others, terror.

When a human mind, spirit, or ego lacks discipline—watch out! Such an individual is apt randomly to erupt in tension-releasing outbursts. For him these acts may dispose of internal personal conflict. Innocent souls in his vicinity, however, are forced to absorb the shock of the exploding passion.

The so-called "free spirit" often wonders why many shun him. He fails to appreciate the emotional cost to others when he insists on flaunting his "freedom."

RESPONSE

Sense warmth, feel a glow. . . .
Kindred soul or artifice?
Instinct should decide.

In a human encounter, when we gain an "instinctive" impression, the response should also be instinctive. Analysis is inconsistent with instinct. In human response, each destroys the other. Here, caution is less a sign of prudence than of immaturity.

The head and the heart each have their function and their jurisdiction. Neither should trespass on the other's domain.

SIGNALS

At one's desk, "I agree!"
Going out the door, shoulders
Send another answer.

The eloquence of a disagreeing subordinate is seldom verbal. A distant look, a suppressed sigh, or, as in this instance, a pinched posture about the shoulders signals that the subordinate thinks otherwise.

We see here the skilled underling using backside body language to rebut his frontside concurrence. The wise superior will observe both and understand the difference.

ANNIVERSARY

*Quite in time for guilt
Yet too late for atonement,
She mentions the day.*

At their peril, males forget occasions of marital sentiment. Lack of attentiveness and a sense of fairness are both masculine weaknesses. When he displays the first, she can fell him with a telling thrust to the second. Can, and often does!

PUBLIC LIFE

Perilous spotlight—
Eagerly he slips into it.
The exit. . . bumpy.

While public life is no bed of roses, men continue to seek it. Public center stage stimulates one's adrenalin, tests one's talents, and fiendishly nurtures the ego. For this, men willingly risk ruthless scrutiny and expose themselves to captious criticism. Yet when, as it must, the spotlight switches off, life often seems strangely incomplete. A period of groping may ensue. Rough.

MORALITY

> *"You erred!" exclaimed "A."*
> *"B" relaxed, oh, so relieved,*
> *Having feared he had sinned.*

The Judeo-Christian concept of sin is largely alien to Oriental thinking. Human mistakes, of course, are acknowledged. To be mistaken is merely to display bad judgment.

To sin, on the other hand, is to reflect bad intent. The world accepts the fallibility of human judgment, but one's intent should be "pure." Hence, the chasmic difference between error and evil.

EMPTINESS

That look? lovely, but. . . .
"Our children are adopted,"
She said; and I knew.

You are at a party among strangers. Your dinner partner is attractive but deep in the eyes something is missing. As the conversation goes forward you search for clues to what-is-it. Sorrow maybe; an injured sensibility, perhaps. Then a comment revealing unfulfillment.

OBSESSION

"Darkness of the heart"
They call it; young spirit crushed
By the hand of love.

Motherly love is hardly unique to Japan, but in that society it becomes so powerful at times as to seem obsessive. The theme of many a Japanese legend reflects this obsession. Excessive mothering is revealed as begetting repressive smothering. The perpetrators are known as "monster mamas."

In the imagery-rich Japanese lexicon we discover a haunting phrases: "darkness of the heart." Even when translated the phrase captures much of the poignancy and paradox of this obsessive maternal behavior.

IDEOLOGUE

His mind—a fierce prism
Bending each entering thought
To preconception.

Nothing blights spirited discourse—the sharing of views—more than the intrusions of an ideologue. He starts, rather than ends, with conclusions. His mind refracts rather than reacts.

Though we admire genuine conviction, we are annoyed by the ideologue's insistent pre-cast insertions. His willingness to distort the views of others is often even more objectionable than his own sterile opinions. Let us banish him.

TIMES

Twilight and autumn—
Next-to-closing is best;
Theater or life.

My favorite times of the day and of the year occur just before their end. One is struck by the fact that, in theatrical drama, the climax usually occurs in the next-to-last scene. In revues, the top performers are given the next-to-closing spot.

It becomes apparent that the theatrical structure created by man merely reflects a sequential pattern he has copied from nature.

AGING

Round roll the seasons
As life's brief circle tightens,
Each year a bit more.

A seventy-five-year-old sentiment here. Anyone on the yonder side of three score and ten knows the feeling.

On the Writing of These Verses

For contemporary, Americans "do it yourself" is less an admonition than a credo. It is almost a disease. One fallout from this infesting virus has been an emergence among Americans of a seemingly insatiable appetite for "how to do" writings on just about everything.

How to write Senryu?* Connoisseurs would regard a treatise by an amateur as a dubious addition to "how to" literature. Whether the composing process can be helpfully dissected is questionable. I suppose the best advice is found in the old Japanese proverb *"Narau yori, narero"*—learn by doing.

Yet I do get asked how, and with what prompting, I wrote these verses. So as an appendix of sorts I thought I might offer a few words on the subject. I'll do this by examining one taken from this volume.

But before I launch into this examination, a comment or two. First, I found that the joy of composing these

---

*Should you really want a learned treatise on this subject, I suggest Kimura Kimmonsen's *How To Write Senryu.*

verses springs from a disciplined adherence to standard form. Some craft is then involved, especially the craftsman's talent for making things fit. Fitting the thought to the form can add immeasurably to the joy of conveying the thought. As Robert Frost might have said, writing Senryu without retaining its singular form would be like playing tennis without a net. Quite simply, it ruins the game.

In my verses I also sought to keep things simple. My goal? Perspective and insight, not profundity. I did not even try to eschew banality, which exists aplenty in these verses. Consider, if you will, the verse labeled "Beauty." Note the unadorned, and I believe even banal, flavor of these lines:

> *The exciting thought*
> *That beauty is possible,*
> *Sustains us all.*

Nothing elegant here. Yet something I thought worth saying is there—particularly the "all" part. The desire to accomplish something "beautiful" is universal. I've never seen why the aesthetically refined should be afforded exclusive jurisdiction over an attribute as wide-ranging as appreciation of beauty.

At best, refinement ranks as an arguable virtue. Chekhov declares flatly that the more refined one is, the more unhappy. Though the rigidity of the dramatist's equation is vulnerable to dissent, there may be at least something to be said for it. So in writing these verses I never sought to reach for refinement if simplicity seemed within grasp.

Finally, I should explain what aficionados may well consider a miscast experiment. While I have adhered to Senryu's structural form, admittedly I have been guilty of adding to it. Giving each verse a title and appending some amplifying comment was strictly my own idea, one, of course, not common to "true" Japanese Senryu. I did this simply because I found the three-way combination of Title, Verse, and Comment to be useful for my particular purposes.

How I Came to Write "Humor"

The blackness of truth
Needs humor's illumination
To lighten one's life.

Originally I contemplated doing a verse solely on the role of humor in public life. My interest was not in the quality of public humor; rather, in its *utility*. The utility of humor in public life was first brought home to me during a Washington evening in the early nineteen seventies. In those days Ambassador Lord Cromer set an uncommonly good table in his elegant British Embassy Residence.

At the Cromer dinner table on the evening in question, a dozen or so of us were engaged in a lively discussion. As sometimes happens the conversation inexplicably sagged for a moment. Sensing the vacuum, up spoke New Jersey Congressman Peter Frelinghysen. Peter offered the assembled gastronomes one of the more incredible comments I've heard from a public figure. And I've heard a number.

"Humor" he announced in void-filling tones, "has *no* place in political life." Just like that! At once a storm of rebuttal erupted, restoring high decibel ratings to the evening's badinage.

Unfortunately I never did have an opportunity to seek out Peter and learn whether his remark carried serious intent or whether he was merely improvising some salty grist for our flagging conversational mill. I rather think the former. The Congressman was hardly a flippant man. He may well have seen public careers shattered by mots that misfired. Or perhaps, like others of us, he might have found himself groaning inwardly as he listened to certain political figures of the time foundering in misguided attempts at show-biz–type humor.

Despite Peter's postulate, however, I have never questioned the welcome role humor plays in public life. I find it easy to agree with Santayana when he insists, "Unmitigated seriousness is always out of place in human affairs."

Among its expert practitioners, humor in public affairs serves many a useful purpose, especially to relieve tension or to puncture inflated egos. As a tool of statecraft, humor can even serve as a spark to ignite international amity. I recall a minor but delightful example of the latter.

In the spring of 1975, Japan's then newly-appointed Foreign Minister Kiichi Miyazawa flew into Washington on his maiden ministerial pilgrimage to that presumed fount of free-world wisdom. In any initial human encounter, it is important that things go well. In the hypersensitive world of diplomacy, what is otherwise important becomes crucial.

On the first day of his visit, the Foreign Minister and I

were scheduled to have a luncheon meeting with Secretary Kissinger in one of those plush eighth-floor State Department dining rooms.

Our timing was bad. We had chosen the very day on which Gerald Ford, the nation's new President, was to give his first foreign-policy address. This meant the Secretary was spending the morning across town in the White House feverishly putting finishing touches to the speech.

Over at Foggy Bottom, we awaited the Secretary's return. It grew late. Noon came and no Henry. Lunch began and still no Henry. The empty chair was chillingly conspicuous. Then along about the fish course the door burst open and in swept the Secretary. Apologizing profusely for his tardiness, Kissinger explained that only moments ago he and the President had finally agreed on the final text. He ended by saying the speech was now being readied for delivery that evening.

The Foreign Minister didn't quite understand and asked, "If you agreed on the text, what more needs to be done with the speech?" Quickly lapsing into his thickest Teutonic accent, Henry shot back, "Tsay are translating it from Tsa original Churman."

The icy atmosphere instantly melted. Mr. Miyazawa and the Secretary went on to become the most amiable of colleagues. Their easy personal relationship became one of the most positive features of our enduring Japanese/American friendship.

What I have been getting around to by the foregoing is a conclusion I soon came to. I decided the ingredients of humor in public life were pretty much the same as humor generally. So I dropped my idea of focusing my verse on political humor.

Having decided to comment on the general utility of humor what was it I wanted to say? Two things, perhaps.

First, I would insist that humor did indeed have utility—a usefulness that extended beyond mere entertainment. Second, I wished to picture humor as valuable, almost necessary, to man's sanity. As James Thurber tells us, "humor improves everything."

Analyzing humor is most unhumorous, but one has to start somewhere. It seemed to me that humor exposed the vagaries of life, the capriciousness of fate, the contrast between dreams and reality, our own personal failings, what we regard as the curious characteristics of others, and so on. With only seventeen syllables to work with, however, all this stuff needed to be boiled down into a single term. I chose the word "Truth."

So I found myself wanting to say something like, "While the truth may hurt, the pain is eased by humor." But of course humor can do more than relieve pain; it can provide insight. Humor often casts a whole new light on things.

With this idea in mind, I went on to the next step, to say something like: "The often unpleasantness of truth needs humor, not only to make it palatable, but to make it understood."

For my "humor," I will only mention one compositional element. I believe the cohesion of this verse, if indeed it has any, lies in the common spectrum of three words "blackness," "illumination," and "lighten."

Stumbling upon the word "lighten" proved particularly felicitous. When much must be said with little, as in Senryu verses, short words with multiple meanings are a godsend. Since I was seeking to show that humor pro-

93

vides both relief and perspective, "lighten" served to convey both. Lighten, of course, means "to throw light on" as well as "to reduce the burden on."

To convey a thought in seventeen meager syllables demands a creative use of language. I found that in writing Senryu rigidity of form inspires—

The blackness of truth
Needs humor's illumination
To lighten one's life.

Bibliography

Books

Blyth, R.H. *Japanese Life and Character in Senryu.* Tokyo: Hokuseido Press, 1969.
——. *Oriental Humor.* Tokyo: Hokuseido Press, 1959.
——. *Senryu.* Tokyo: Hokuseido Press, 1949.
Brown, J.C. "Senryu: Poems of the People." Tokyo: Charles E. Tuttle Co., 1990.
Enki, Naruni. *Senryu: Short Witty Odes.* Tokyo: Makita Ronoi, 1924.
Henderson, Harold J. *The Throat of the Peacock* (a book of modern senryu). Matsuyama, Japan: Seki Publishing Co., Ltd., 1974.
Kimura, Kimmonsen. *How to Write Senryu.* N.p., n.d.

Articles

Blyth, R.H. "Buddhism in Senryu, I." *The Young East* 19:6–10 (Autumn 1956).

——. "Buddhism in Senryu, II." *The Young East* 20:17–20 (Winter 1956).

——. "Haiku, Senryu, Zen." *Japan Quarterly* 9(1): 76–81 (January/March 1964).

——. "The Position of Haiku and Senryu in World Literature." *Contemporary Japan* 19:537–51 (1950).

——. "Senryu, I." *Kokusai Bunka Shinkokai Bulletin* 20:5–7 (September/October 1956).

——. "Senryu, II." *Kokusai Bunka Shinkokai Bulletin* 21:1–3 (November/December 1956).

——. "Why Nobody Likes Senryu." *Orient/West* 7(3): 11–13 (March 1962).

Harr, Lorraine Ellis. "Senryu: Humor in the Japanese Satirical Poetry." *Ikebana International Quarterly* (1986).

Hoyt, Clement. "Haiku and Senryu." *American Haiku* 1(2): 1–8 (1963).

Johnston, Thomas. "Insight and Awareness in Senryu and Haiku." *American Haiku* 3(2): 56–60 (1965).

Sadler, A.W. "From a Senryu Notebook." *Japan Quarterly* 12(1): 85–86 (January/March 1965).